All About Friends

friends

Contents

4-5 What are friends?

6-7 Why do we need friends?

8-9 What makes good friends?

10-11 Who can be friends?

12-13 Making friends

14-15 Friends together

16-17 Friendship groups

18-19 How NOT to be friends

20-21 When friends fall out

22-23 Friends and feelings

24-25 Playing fair

26-27 Ways to fix things

28-29 Changing and growing

30 Friends puzzle

31-32 Notes for grown-ups

Francesca and Olivia

Charlie and Marcel

Otto and Rufus

Usborne
All About Friends

Felicity Brooks

Illustrated by Mar Ferrero

Designed by Frankie Allen

forever friends

Isobel and Jack

I'm Mar and these are my friends, Arancha and Carmen.

Hi! I'm Felicity. This is my friend Paula.

I'm Frankie and this is my friend Holly. She makes me laugh.

What are friends?

It can be fun to spend time by yourself. You can play whatever you want and you don't have to share your toys . . . or your snacks.

But some things are not so fun by yourself. And that's when it is good to have friends.

Hmmm

Friends SHARE all sorts of things such as . . .

Want a go?

. . . toys

Shall we play the robot game?

YES!

. . . games

Do you want one?

Yes, please.

. . . treats

I'm feeling a bit sad today.

Oh dear!

. . . feelings

Whisper, whisper: I've made this for my dad's birthday!

and even secrets.

Friends often enjoy
doing the same things.

Friends look forward
to seeing each other.

They help each other
and listen to each other.

They say nice things
about each other.

They might make
each other laugh.

And they like each other
just the way they are.

But most of all, friends make each other feel happy. Any children can
be your friends if they are nice to you and want to play with you.

Why do we need friends?

Long, long ago when there were no shops, friends were useful to help you find food and water. That's probably why people first made friends.

A friend could also help you stay away from danger.

And friends still help us ...

... and help us stay safe.

But good friends do a lot more, too. They help us to learn things and make us feel good about ourselves.

They help us learn to WORK TOGETHER.

They help us learn to SHARE and TAKE TURNS.

They help us to THINK about other people's FEELINGS.

They help us learn to PLAY NICELY together.

They help us learn to BE KIND to each other.

They help us learn to FORGIVE each other when we make mistakes.

Friends CHEER each other up.

They STOP us from feeling bored.

They help us FIND OUT things.

They SUPPORT us when we have to do something difficult.

Can you think of some other reasons why it's good to have friends? You could write your own list and draw some pictures.

What makes good friends?

There is no such thing as a perfect friend, but you can be good friends if you do these things most of the time.

OK, it's hide and seek!

You agree together what to play.

You take turns.

Weeeee!

What's your favourite animal?

A dolphin

Mine too!

You ask questions (and listen to the answers).

That's really good!

Thank you!

You say nice things to each other.

I've run out of water.

You can have some of mine!

You help each other sort out problems.

You help each other when one is upset.

You are kind and polite to each other.

You stand up for each other if someone else is unkind.

If you fall out, you find ways to make up.

You show that you are pleased to see each other.

You share things.

What do you think makes a good friend? If you have a friend, can you think of three nice things about him or her?

Who can be friends?

All kinds of people can be friends. Friends can be . . .

very young

very old

and everything in between.

Friends can be . . .

tall   short

big   small

Frankie!

HELLO! How are YOU?

Very well, thank you.

noisy   quiet

Like my new glasses?

They're a bit big.

funny   serious

busy

relaxed

or sporty

Some like bright colours. Some prefer dark. Some like pets ... and some don't.

Some really, really love dinosaurs.

Some really can't stand them ...

... and some just want to be dinosaurs.

Friends can be the same age, different ages, and from different places.

If you have a grandparent, or know an older person, ask them about their friends. How long have they been friends? How did they meet?

Making friends

If you want to make a new friend, how do you do it? Often the hardest part is starting to talk to someone for the first time. It helps if you make yourself look like someone who is friendly.

Which of these looks most friendly to you?

Head down

Not looking at you

Not talking

Arms folded into body

Not smiling

Body drooping

Hello!

Head up

Looking at you

Smiling face

Saying hello

Arms wide

Standing up tall

So, to look friendly, it's a good idea to look at someone, smile, and then say 'hi' or 'hello' (and say the other person's name, if you know it).

Hello! My name's Ravi.

I have two cats.

Do you have any pets?

You could introduce yourself (say what your name is).

Then, you could say something about yourself.

You could ask the other person a question.

You could offer to join in with something . . .

. . . or to help them with something.

Or ask about how they are feeling.

You could say something nice about them.

You could do something kind.

You could ask them to join in with a game.

New friends can find out a lot about each other by asking questions. Here's what Ravi now knows about Asha.

Many children feel shy when they first meet new people, but finding a way to start talking can really help you make new friends.

Friends together

When you are with a friend or a group of friends, there are all kinds of things you can do together.

This is my friend Kylie.

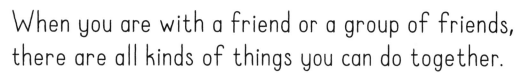

Make up a game or a dance routine.

Invite your friends to meet your family. (Don't forget to introduce them.)

Plant some seeds.

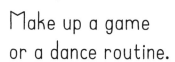

SOB! SOB!

Help each other when things are difficult or sad.

WEEEE!

Bounce on a trampoline.

Look after pets.

COOL!

Look at a book together.

I am CAPTAIN of this ship!

Put on a play.

Build something.

Make cards for your friends' birthdays.

SIX!

Play a board game.

Ha ha HAA

HEE HEE hee

Watch a film together.

A friend is someone you choose to be with and who likes to be with you. You feel happy most of the time when you are with friends.

Friendship groups

You can have more than one good friend and more than one group of friends. You might have a group of friends at school, some friends at home, some family friends or some friends you do an activity with.

"These are my cousins and we go cycling together at weekends."

"We are all in the same class at school."

"We all go to an after-school club."

"Our mums are friends and we are, too."

"We all play football together."

You don't have to play with the same friend or the same group every day. Playing in different groups is good for all kinds of reasons.

If one person can't play, there are always others to play with.

You can play all kinds of different games.

You can make a team to play another team.

One two THREE four!

Phoebe!

In a group of three, if one person feels left out, or two fight over one friend, you could ask another person to join you, to see if this evens things out.

How NOT to be friends

When friends are not kind to each other, they can make each other feel unhappy or upset. These are some of the things a NOT-GOOD friend might do.

Not listen to what you say or interrupt you all the time.

Which animal do you like best?

Well, I like . . .

I LIKE ELEPHANTS BECAUSE THEY HAVE REALLY BIG EARS AND I LIKE THEIR HUGE FEET AND THEIR WRINKLY SKIN AND I ALSO LIKE ZEBRAS BECAUSE THEY...

SIGH!

I've got MILLIONS of toys at home and I've got THIRTEEN bikes and I'm the BEST dancer in the school and MY DAD has been to the MOON!

Tease you, make fun of you or call you names.

You're a silly poo-head!

Boast about things or tell lies.

Blame you for things which are not your fault.

Boss you around all the time and not say 'please' or 'thank you'.

Say mean things about you to other children . . .

Not share toys.

. . . or agree with other children who say mean things.

Play too roughly, yelling, hitting or hurting you.

Are YOU ever a not-good friend? If you think you sometimes might be, can you think of ways you could be kinder to your friends?

When friends fall out

Even good friends sometimes fall out. They may argue, disagree or annoy each other and then don't want to be together for a while. This can make them feel upset, but it doesn't mean they can't stay friends.

Sometimes friends fall out because they can't agree about something.

It's MY turn!
NO, it's mine!

You ate the last one?

THAT WAS MINE!

That's NOT funny!

This is a STUPID game!

NOT FAIR!

Sometimes friends fall out because one doesn't understand how the other is feeling.

Now let's spin around really, really FAST!

I don't want to. I feel...

Aran

Arthur

You NEVER want to do FUN things!
I'm going to play with Oscar.

But... but... boo hoo, bleurrrgh!

That's why it's always a good idea to TALK with your friends about how you are feeling. Here's what Arthur could say so he doesn't hurt Aran's feelings.

Arthur
Are you OK? You look a bit funny!

Aran
I like the spinning game. But it makes me feel *sick*.

Arthur
OK, I'm sorry. I'll get your mum.

Here, Arthur and Aran didn't fall out because Arthur noticed that Aran wasn't feeling well. He asked him about it and helped him and Aran didn't get upset.

Friends and feelings

It can really help you NOT to fall out with friends if you can notice and talk about how you are feeling. How do you think these children are feeling? Match the words to the pictures.

Sad	Happy	Cold	Worried	Angry
Unwell	Shy	Excited	Hot	Tired

These are some questions you could ask to find out how a friend is feeling.

What's the matter?

Are you OK?

What's wrong?

How are you feeling?

Do you need some help?

If someone is hurting your feelings or annoying you, first you could try asking them politely to stop, starting with the word 'please'. Then, let them know how you feel starting with the word 'I'.

"Please, could you stop saying that.
I don't find it funny."

"Please, don't ignore me.
I'd like to join in."

"Please, stop pushing me.
I find it really annoying."

"Please, be quiet!
I can't hear the story."

Can you think of a time when someone was hurting your feelings or annoying you? What could you say if this happened again?

Playing fair

It's best not to fall out with friends in the first place, and playing together in a fair way can really help. These are some ideas to try.

Agree on something everbody wants to do.
(It might not be what you want at first).

Share things out fairly and remember to take turns.

Make sure everyone knows the rules of a game before you start.

Think of ways to change the game if it's not working well.

DON'T cheat and don't spoil a game if you don't like it or are not winning.

Remember that if a friend wants to play with someone else sometimes, it doesn't mean they are not your friend any more. Even best friends don't have to play together all the time.

A fair way to choose who is 'it', who goes first, or who goes out, is to use a rhyme such as 'Eeny, meeny, miney, moe' or 'Ip, dip, sky blue'.

Who's . . . it? . . . Not . . . YOU!

Highest number starts!

Heads or tails?

Longest goes first!

Or you could roll a dice . . .

flip a coin . . .

. . . or choose sticks or straws.

If you and a friend just can't agree about something, you can 'agree to disagree' and still stay friends.

It's important to have your own ideas. You don't have to agree about everything.

I like cats.

I like dogs.

But we both like pizza!

Ways to fix things

If you do fall out with a friend and it is making you unhappy, there is a lot you can do to try to fix things.

Take a little TIME away from each other so you both cool down. When you feel ready, go back to your friend in a kind way. If you have made a mistake, you need to say SORRY.

> I'm sorry I didn't want to play with you when you felt sick. Can we play something else?

> That's OK. You didn't know I felt sick.

> Shall we play the dinosaur game instead?

TIPS FOR SAYING SORRY

1. Say clearly what you are sorry about.

2. Be serious and make sure you mean it.

3. Don't say it in a jokey or grumpy way.

4. Suggest a way to make things better.

If a friend has made a mistake and they say sorry to you, make sure you tell them it's OK and FORGIVE them.

> That's OK. You didn't mean to and my dad can mend it.

> I'm really sorry I ripped your top!

If someone keeps annoying you or is never a good friend, try not to shout at them, hit or kick out.

1 2 3 4 5 6 7 8 9 10

Move away from them, if you can, and take a very deep breath.

Count slowly to 10 in your head as you breathe out through your mouth. Then do all this again.

You could try playing with someone else for a while and wait to see if your friend tries to fix things with you.

Remember that if anyone . . .

- is mean to you all the time
- often hurts your feelings
- does unkind things on purpose
- says mean things about you to other children

- agrees with others who are being unkind
- hurts, hits, kicks, bites or punches you
- makes fun of you or calls you names
- leaves you out of things all the time
- takes, damages or hides your things

. . . that person is NOT your friend and you need to tell a grown-up such as a teacher, parent or carer about what is going on.

grrrr

Sometimes you can't fix things and that's OK. Sometimes people just can't get along so they have to let a friendship go and move on.

27

Changing and growing

All friendships go through ups and downs as friends grow and change. Friendships can change in all kinds of ways. Friends may . . .

move away from each other . . .   break apart   . . . or stay friends

When you are young, your friends may change quite often. It can be sad if a friendship ends, but losing one friend can make room for a new friendship to grow. And it just might be one that lasts a long time.

Kirsty and Ali at preschool

Kirsty and Ali's first day at big school

Kirsty with the happy couple at Ali and Rani's wedding

Kirsty and Ali's children meet

Kirsty and Ali's Holidays

Kirsty and Ali photos 1

Kirsty and Ali photos 2

Kirsty and Ali photos 3

Kirsty and Ali photos 4

Remember that not everyone has to be your friend and not everyone has to like you. You DON'T need lots and lots of friends to stay happy.

You can have all sorts of different kinds of friends in your life and they don't always have to be children. Grown-ups who you know well can be friends too.

"Here's me and Grandpa at the seaside."

"This is me and my auntie Emma in a boat."

"Me and my childminder Claudia at the zoo."

Friends don't even have to be people!

This is my fairy friend Amy.

Some children imagine a friend that other people can't see.

MEOW!

WOOF, WOOF!

Many people say that their pets are their friends.

Tea, Bunny?

A lot of little children think of their toys as friends . . .

. . . or their cuddly blankets

. . . or even their vacuum cleaners!

Friendship puzzle

How much can you remember about being a good friend? For each of these little stories about friends, choose a kind thing to do or say.

Mala has been playing with a toy for a long time and Holly wants a turn. What should Holly do?

Snatch the toy.

Say, 'Please, can I have a turn next?'

Cry.

Jess has built a high tower but Aisha knocks it down by mistake. What should Aisha do?

Say, 'It was a stupid tower anyway.'

Laugh.

Say, 'sorry' and help Jess build it again.

Sam wants to make friends with a new boy called Mo. What should Sam do?

Say, 'I don't like your coat.'

Say, 'Hello, my name's Sam. What's yours?'

Say, 'I'm the best footballer in the world.'

Yasmin is looking upset. What should her friend Tandi do?

Push Yasmin.

Play with someone else.

Ask, 'What's the matter?'

Charlie has lost his pencil and asks Ivan to help him. What should Ivan do?

Say, 'You're silly to lose your pencil.'

Say, 'Go away! I'm busy.'

Say, 'I'll help you to look for it.'

Some notes for grown-ups

Friendship has a huge impact on children's physical and mental wellbeing. It builds their self-esteem and helps them to start finding out who they are outside their family, as well as allowing them to develop essential life skills. Friends help children build mental resilience, learn how to cope with disappointment and deal with problems. Most importantly, friendship helps children develop empathy (the ability to imagine how others are feeling), encouraging them to start moving beyond self-interest to consider the needs of others.

This book is designed to help children think and talk about what friendship is, and to develop the skills required to make and maintain good friendships. These skills include:

taking turns	communication	cooperation
sharing	negotiation	persuasion
being kind	problem-solving	compromise
being polite	recognizing others' feelings	forgiveness
considering others' needs	conflict resolution	empathy

Like other skills, these all need plenty of practice and there is a lot that adults can do to help:

• If your child is shy and finds it hard to initiate friendships, rehearse the 'scripts' on page 12 for greeting and meeting — smiling, making eye contact, saying 'hello' and the other child's name, etc.

• Talk about the 'ingredients' of friendship such as greeting and giving compliments; sharing interests, toys and games; being kind and polite, etc.

• Help your child recognize behaviours that may push other children away — appearing withdrawn, disrupting games, arguing, being bossy or aggressive, ignoring 'stop signals', boasting, lying, being a poor sport (arguing, cheating, etc.).

• Encourage children to join activities where they may make friends with children with similar interests, but respect your child's personality: some children need a lot of friends while others may not need as many to feel happy.

• Talk about friendships within your family. Who is Grandma's friend? Does Dad have friends?

• Support children by arranging play dates, inviting their friends to your home, if you can, and talking beforehand about what they could do together.

• Talk about nice things to do to make sure the guest has a good time: introducing people; going along with what the guest wants to do; trying not to argue; staying with the guest and not wandering away; offering the guest a drink.

• If you can, encourage any shared interests by providing the resources needed such as paper, crayons, games, toys, books, films, etc.

• Teach children some of the 'playing fair' techniques shown on page 25 such as counting out rhymes, picking straws, flipping coins, rolling dice, listening, taking turns and sharing out equally.

• Role-play apologizing and accepting an apology if your child has fallen out with a friend — look at page 26 and stress that an apology must be sincere and not done in a jokey or grumpy way.

• Talk about diversity with your child – how everyone is different and that's a positive thing; it's good to have things in common, but also to respect differences.

• Make children aware that friendships may take effort and they can sometimes be challenging and frustrating as well as enjoyable, exciting and fun.

• Read all kinds of stories together, not only happy ones. Talking about difficult emotions in books is a very good way to build empathy.

• Children learn from your example so try to be a good role model in valuing your own friendships and demonstrating politeness, kindness and empathy.

Dealing with conflicts

When conflicts occur, it's important to give children the opportunity to sort things out themselves in the first instance (except in cases of bullying or violence where swift intervention is necessary). Getting through arguments can strengthen friendships, but bear in mind that children's feelings change quickly and what may seem like the end of the world one day is often almost forgotten the next. At this age, arguments are normal and frequent – children argue much more with their friends than with other children – but listen to your child's concerns when they talk about friendship problems. However trivial they may seem to you, they are important to your child and even though early years' friendships generally don't last long, young children become very attached to their friends and we should do what we can to nurture their friendships.

We can also help children to understand that friendships should be reciprocal and respectful so that they recognize when someone is being a 'not-good' friend. Parents and carers can role-model kind behaviour, forgiving and not bearing grudges, but continually tolerating and excusing mean or aggressive behaviour damages self-esteem. We can help children understand that if they can't fix things, it is time to let go and move on.

Imaginary friends

Parents and carers are sometimes worried about their children having imaginary friends, but studies show there is no cause for concern. These kinds of friends are most common among 3 to 5 year-olds, especially for first-born and only children, and by the age of 7, nearly 40 per cent of children report having had an imaginary friend. In studies, children with such a friend were found to be generally more socially aware, more empathetic, more creative, more able to focus on minds rather than looks, and had a better understanding of self.

Usborne Quicklinks
Visit Usborne Quicklinks for links to websites about children and friendships, with activities and video clips to share with them. There is also helpful advice about what to do if you think your child is being bullied or is bullying others.

Go to Usborne.com/Quicklinks and type in the keywords 'all about friends'. Children should be supervised online. Please read our internet safety guidelines at the Usborne Quicklinks website.

Usborne Publishing is not responsible for the availability or content of any website other than its own, or for any exposure to harmful, offensive or inaccurate material which may appear on the Web.